My Pet

GERBIL

Kate Petty

Stargazer Books

Gerbils as pets

The first pet gerbils came from the Mongolian desert, where they live in underground burrows. They have long tails and strong hind legs, like tiny kangaroos.

Other rodent pets, such as hamsters and mice, wake up at night, but gerbils like to play in the daytime. They are fun to keep and easy to tame. Gerbils live for three to four years.

A Mongolian gerbil in its natural home

A young Mongolian gerbil ▶

All sorts of gerbils

Most pet gerbils are "agoutis" and are the same sandy color as wild gerbils. But now you can buy them in different colors, too. There are black ones and white ones and beautiful silver-gray varieties.

A few pet shops sell Egyptian gerbils. They are smaller than Mongolian gerbils but make equally good pets.

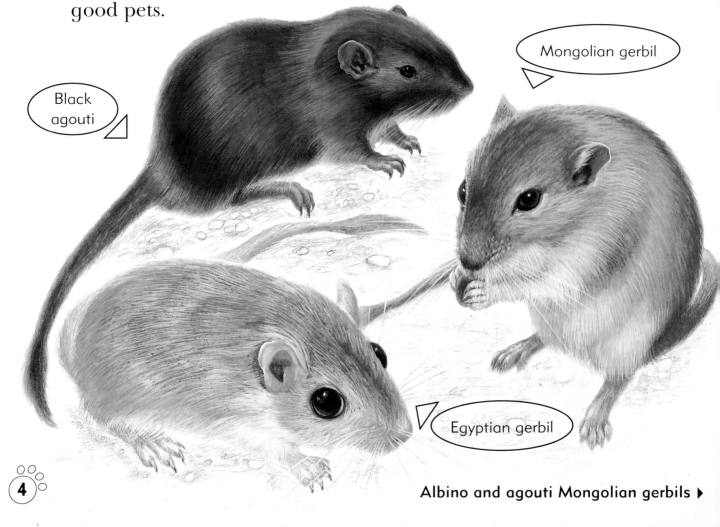

Black agouti

Mongolian gerbil

Egyptian gerbil

Albino and agouti Mongolian gerbils ▶

A closer look

A male gerbil is about four inches (10 cm) high and weighs about five ounces (130 g). Females are smaller —about three inches (7 cm). With their large eyes and sensitive ears, gerbils can see and hear all around them.

A gerbil's long, fur-covered tail helps it to balance. If an enemy pounces on it, the fur comes off and the gerbil escapes. But the fur never grows again.

The fur-covered tail of this white gerbil is quite different from the tail of a mouse or a hamster.

Gerbils have large, bright eyes and long whiskers. ▶

Jumpers

Gerbils are fantastic jumpers. Their back legs are extra strong and they can leap away from danger very fast. They can even manage a vertical take-off.

Pet gerbils are very nimble and hard to catch if they escape. They often stand up on their hind legs to get a better view of their surroundings.

A gray agouti gerbil jumping

A gerbil stretched to its full height to take a look around ▶

Eating

Pet gerbils only need to be fed once a day. They eat a mixture of grains and enjoy a few dandelion leaves or fresh vegetables. A carrot or a piece of wood to gnaw on keeps their teeth from growing too long.

Although gerbils are desert animals, and need very little to drink, they must always have a supply of fresh water.

A feast for a lilac gerbil includes grains, seeds, hay, fresh fruit and vegetables, and some raisins.

An Egyptian gerbil keeping his teeth in trim ▶

Sociable gerbils

Gerbils like company, so it is best to keep two or more together. But beware—gerbils that are strangers fight, and can even kill each other.

A male and female gerbil kept together will reproduce babies very quickly. So gerbils that are going to share a cage must be either all brothers or all sisters.

Black-patched gerbils starting to fight

Gerbils from the same litter will stay friends. ▶

The burrowers

Gerbils need to be able to burrow and tunnel if they are to be happy. They can be kept in cages with wire bars, but a "gerbilarium" is the best home for them.

This can be made from a fish tank. It gives plenty of room for the six inches (15 cm) of burrowing material gerbils need, and you can watch them through the sides of the tank.

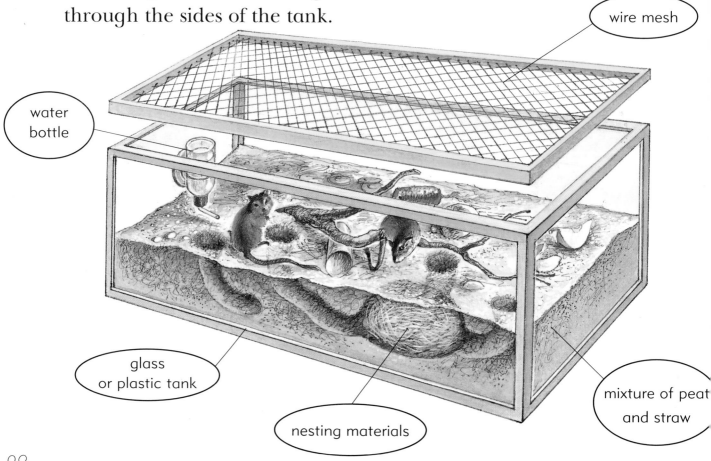

wire mesh

water bottle

glass or plastic tank

nesting materials

mixture of peat and straw

Mongolian gerbils asleep in a burrow ▶

Newborn gerbils

Gerbil parents stay together for life and the father helps to care for the family. The babies are born 24 days after mating. As the parents can produce another new family every 24 days, it is sensible to separate them in captivity.

There are usually four or five babies, and they are born blind and hairless. It is important not to disturb them for the first few days.

Newborn gerbils are about 1 inch (3 cm) long, the same length as a matchstick.

These Egyptian gerbils' fur appeared when they were five days old. ▶

Growing up

The babies grow up very quickly. They start to explore the nest when they are only a week old, although their eyes won't open until the tenth or twelfth day.

They carry on drinking milk from their mother until they are four weeks old. At this stage they are ready to go to new homes. After three months, gerbils are fully grown.

Three-week-old babies start eating grains.

Young Egyptian gerbils playing ▶

Handle with care

Gerbils are nervous little creatures, so it is worth taking time and trouble to make friends. One hand must always support the gerbil's weight when it is lifted.

A gerbil can be gently picked up by the base of its tail, but never, ever by the tip. If the gerbil "freezes" with fright, put it back in its cage.

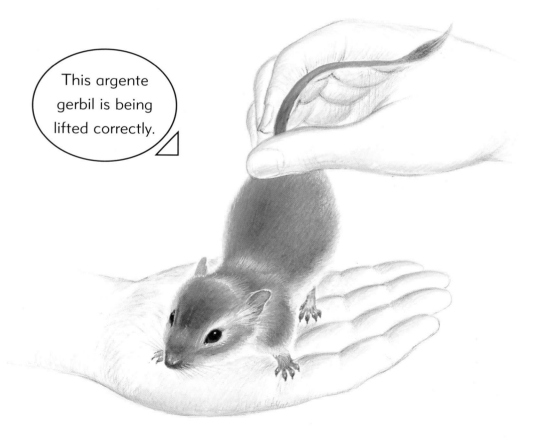

This argente gerbil is being lifted correctly.

Gerbils like funny places to hide in. ▶

Know your gerbils

A few pet stores sell Egyptian gerbils, but most pet-owners keep Mongolian gerbils. There is a variety of different colored Mongolian gerbils to choose from.

Select your pet carefully. You can recognize a healthy gerbil by its bright eyes, glossy coat, and its inquisitive nature.

Agouti gerbil

Black gerbil

Albino gerbil

Index

©Aladdin Books Ltd 2006

Produced by **Aladdin Books Ltd**

First published in the
United States in 2006 by
Stargazer Books
c/o The Creative Company
123 South Broad Street
P.O. Box 227
Mankato, Minnesota 56002

Designer: Pete Bennett – PBD
Editor: Rebecca Pash
Illustrator: George Thompson
Picture Research: Cee Weston-Baker

Printed in Malaysia

Photographic credits:
All photographs supplied by Bruce Coleman,
except cover: PBD

Library of Congress Cataloging-in-Publication Data

Petty, Kate.
    Gerbil / by Kate Petty.
       p. cm. -- (My pet)
    Includes index.
    ISBN 1-59604-030-0
       1. Gerbils as pets--Juvenile literature.
       I. Title.

SF459.G4P465 2005
636.935'83--dc22
                                    2004064984